# Specialties

## of the House

GREAT RECIPES THAT GUESTS ASK FOR

CHOSEN FROM EIGHT OF AMERICA'S

MOST ADMIRED AND POPULAR

COOKBOOKS, AS SELECTED BY AND

SERVED TO THE DELIGHTED GUESTS

OF ELIZABETH H. GROSSMAN

WITH DECORATIONS BY

JOHN ALCORN

SIMON AND SCHUSTER, NEW YORK

Recipes in *Specialties of the House* were selected from the following cookbooks:

*Twelve Company Dinners,* copyright © 1957 by Margo Rieman

*House & Garden's Cook Book,* copyright © 1956, 1957, 1958 by Condé Nast Publications, Inc.

*The Fireside Cook Book,* copyright 1949 by Simon and Schuster, Inc.

*The New Settlement Cook Book,* copyright 1954 by The Settlement Cook Book Co.

*VIP Tosses a Party,* copyright © 1959 by Virgil Partch and William McIntyre

*The Breakfast Cook Book,* copyright © 1959 by Alan Jackson

*The Wonderful World of Cooking,* copyright © 1956 by Edward Harris Heth

*The Art of French Cooking,* copyright © 1958 by Simon and Schuster, Inc.

LIBRARY OF CONGRESS CATALOG CARD NUMBER: 60-14281
MANUFACTURED IN THE UNITED STATES OF AMERICA

# *Contents*

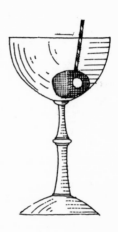

*Page*

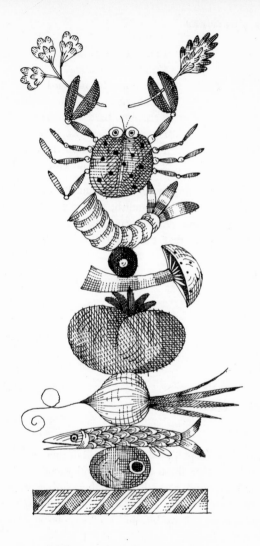

*Hors d'Oeuvres*

*Thirst
Inviter*

1 large clove garlic
1 pint sour cream
1 teaspoon dry mustard
1 tablespoon grated horseradish
2 chopped hard-cooked eggs
1 green pepper, chopped
1 tablespoon chopped parsley
2 tablespoons chili sauce

Grate garlic and blend with sour cream. Beat in with a wooden spoon dry mustard, horseradish, and eggs. Blend in parsley, green pepper, and chili sauce. Allow to stand for 2 hours before serving so that the flavors become blended with the cream.

*Swedish
Meatballs in
Chafing Dish*

[SERVES 6]

This dish can be prepared before cocktail time. Ask the butcher to grind together three times ½ pound round steak, ¼ pound veal and ¼ pound pork. Rub together with a wooden spoon until the meat mixture is very fine, slowly adding to it a piece of white bread, bit by bit, and a tablespoon or two of cream.

Also mix in salt, pepper, a touch of ground allspice, and ¼ teaspoon nutmeg. Shape into very small balls, dust with flour, and brown gently in fresh bacon fat. Add as little water as will prevent them from burning, cover, and simmer as slowly as possible for about 20 minutes. Separately brown ½ pound chicken livers in butter. Also cook in butter ½ pound halved mushroom caps for 5 minutes. Salt lightly.

Put meatballs, livers and mushrooms, with their juices, in the chafing dish. When ready to serve, add ¼ cup dry red wine and simmer all together for 10 minutes. Just before serving, stir in ½ cup sour cream.

## Seveche

Use any lean white fish, or fish and shellfish mixture. Slice and cut into medium-size pieces any combination of raw fish and sea food. Put into shallow dish and spread out so that every piece can be well covered with lime or lemon juice (lime is preferable and traditional). Let stand for at least an hour. When fish is "cooked" in acid of the juice, drain juice off into another bowl. Chop 1 onion and 2 firm tomatoes. Season with salt and pepper and dash of oregano. To ⅓ cup olive oil, add 2 tablespoons of lime juice from fish, seasonings, finely chopped onion and tomato. Mix with fish. Chill and serve as salad or as sea-food cocktail with sauce. This is also ideal served on half of an avocado.

### Pickled Shrimp

[SERVES 8]

2½ pounds shrimp in the shell
½ cup chopped celery
3½ tablespoons salt
¼ cup pickling spices
2½ teaspoons celery seed
2½ tablespoons capers and juice
2 dashes Tabasco
4 large onions
1¼ cups salad oil
¾ cup white vinegar
1½ teaspoons salt

Cook shrimp in 3 quarts boiling water with celery, pickling spices and 3½ tablespoons salt for 5 minutes.

Prepare marinade: Combine 1¼ cups salad oil, white vinegar, salt, celery seed, capers and juice and Tabasco.

Shell shrimp, slice onions into rings. Place layer of onion, then layer of shrimp, and repeat until all are used, in large bowl. Stir marinade and pour over. Let stand 24 hours.

### Crab-Meat Appetizers

[SERVES 8]

Drain contents of a can of crab meat, remove bits of shell, then mix with a can of condensed cream of mushroom soup. Heat this mixture, then add 1 tablespoon of chopped pimento, 1 tablespoon of chopped green pepper, ¼ teaspoon of salt and a little cayenne. Mix. Remove from stove and stir in 1 tablespoon of sherry. Spread on small white bread rounds, sprinkle with bread crumbs and place under broiler until toasted. Serve instantly, while piping hot.

*Baked*
*Stuffed*
*Mushrooms*

24 large mushrooms
1 clove garlic
¼ cup minced parsley
¼ cup Swiss cheese
Salt, pepper
½ cup bread crumbs
2 tablespoons minced onion
¼ cup sherry
Lemon juice
3 tablespoons butter

Wash mushrooms and remove stems, leaving caps intact. Sprinkle a few drops of lemon juice in each cap and set aside. Prepare stuffing by mincing stems very fine, and sautéing in butter. While they cook, grate Swiss cheese into a bowl and add bread crumbs. Mince parsley, garlic and onion. Add to stuffing. Add sherry. When minced stems are browned, add to stuffing, stir thoroughly. Pile this filling into mushroom caps, sprinkle with more bread crumbs and dot with butter. Bake 15 minutes in 350° oven.

11

## Guacamole

2 avocados
⅛-inch slice onion, minced
¼ teaspoon salt
1 clove garlic
Mayonnaise
4 strips bacon
2 dashes Tabasco
¼ teaspoon chili powder
Pepper

Fry 4 strips bacon until crisp, crumble and set aside. Mash 2 ripe avocados, then add 1 finely minced slice of onion, 2 dashes Tabasco, salt, pepper, chili powder and 1 finely minced garlic clove. Stir all together well, put into a small bowl, and cover top completely with mayonnaise so that no air reaches avocado. Just before serving, stir mayonnaise and crumbled bacon bits into the avocado mixture.

## Cheese Wafers

Mix together 1 cup flour and 1¼ cups grated sharp Cheddar cheese. Cut into this ¼ pound butter as you would for any pie dough. Roll the dough into a long sausage about the thickness of a quarter, wrap in wax paper and chill several hours in the refrigerator; the dough will, for that matter, keep for a week or two. When needed, slice off the wafers thinly, as you would icebox cookies, and bake in a moderate oven on a lightly greased cooky sheet until golden tan, about 10 minutes. These are delicious. For variation I sometimes add 1 or 2 tablespoons minced ham to the dough, or 1 tablespoon finely chopped parsley or chives. Or the wafers may be sprinkled with caraway or celery seed before baking.

*Cheese-Onion Pie (Quiche Lorraine)*

[SERVES 8]

Pie crust
½ pound Swiss cheese
2 tablespoons flour
Salt, pepper
3 eggs
3 medium onions or 4 slices bacon
Butter
1 cup milk

Line an 8-inch pie pan with crust. Turn oven to 325° (slow). Sauté 3 medium onions, thinly sliced, in butter and arrange in crust-lined pan. Grate ½ pound Swiss cheese into a bowl. Add 1 tablespoon flour, ¾ teaspoon salt and a dash of pepper. Beat 3 eggs and slowly add 1 cup hot milk. Add cheese and blend well. Pour into unbaked shell and bake in slow (325°) oven for 40 minutes or until a silver knife inserted in the center comes out clean. Do not overbake. Serve warm. (For traditional Quiche Lorraine: Omit onions in above recipe and, instead, spread 4 slices cooked, crumbled bacon over crust-lined pan before pouring cheese-egg mixture in.)

13

## *Avignon Rolls*

[SERVES 6]

Pancake batter
3 tablespoons butter
3 tablespoons flour
1 cup chicken stock
1 cup rich milk
Salt and pepper
½ teaspoon Worcestershire sauce
1 teaspoon dry mustard
1 large can sliced mushrooms
1 cup diced ham
2 tablespoons brandy
2 tablespoons chopped parsley
4 tablespoons grated sharp Cheddar

Make a thin pancake batter from your favorite recipe or follow directions on box of prepared pancake mix. Let it stand while making the filling. Melt the butter and blend in the flour. Stir in the stock and when smooth, add the milk. Stir until the sauce thickens. Season with salt, pepper, Worcestershire sauce and dry mustard. Simmer for 10 minutes. Remove from the stove and measure out ½ cup. Add the mushrooms, ham and brandy to the remaining sauce. Let this cool. Make the pancakes about 5 inches in diameter (allow 3 for each serving). Spread a tablespoonful of ham-mushroom mixture in the center of each thin pancake, leaving a margin around the edge. Roll and place seam side down in a buttered baking dish. Mix the rest of the sauce with the parsley, spread it over the rolled pancakes and bake in a 325° oven for 30 minutes. During the last 5 minutes, sprinkle with grated cheese and brown under the broiler.

14

## Swiss Fondue

¾ pound natural (not processed) imported
    Swiss cheese
1¾ cup white wine (dry, not sweet)
3 teaspoons cornstarch
1 clove garlic
3 tablespoons kirschwasser liqueur
    (optional)

Put the dry white wine in an earthenware casserole or chafing dish that has been rubbed inside with a clove of garlic. Heat wine to boiling point, then add the cheese that has been grated. Stir constantly with a wooden spoon until cheese is creamy. Adjust heat to keep mixture barely simmering. Add the cornstarch (mixed with the kirschwasser if the liqueur is available—otherwise mixed with water) and continue stirring until the mixture bubbles. Add ground pepper to taste.

The Fondue is put in the middle of the dinner table within easy reach of the guests. A platter of toasted, bite-sized chunks of French bread should also be put within easy reach of the guests so they can spear a piece of bread on a fork and dip it into the Fondue.

The casserole of Fondue should be kept hot for second helpings by placing it over an alcohol burner with a low flame. If it becomes too thick add a little wine.

The above quantity is sufficient for a solid first course for six. If Fondue is to be served as a main course, with salad, double above quantities.

15

## Water and Bacon Chestnuts

Wrap small pieces (approximately half-inch cubes) of water chestnut in bacon, then skewer on toothpicks. Broil a few minutes until bacon is cooked. Serve immediately, while hot.

## Vitello Tonnato

[SERVES 10–12]

1 large onion
2 cloves
3 pounds rolled veal
2 bay leaves
2 carrots
2 stalks celery
6 sprigs parsley
2 teaspoons salt
½ teaspoon freshly ground black pepper
2 cans (7 ounce size) tuna fish
1 can anchovy fillets
1 cup olive oil
3 tablespoons lemon juice
1 tablespoon chopped capers

Stud the onion with the cloves. Put in a saucepan with the veal, bay leaves, carrots, celery, parsley, salt, pepper; add water to cover. Cover and cook over medium heat for 2 hours or until veal is tender. Drain and cool. Force the tuna fish and anchovies through a sieve or purée in an electric blender. Beat in the olive oil and lemon juice gradually until very creamy and smooth. Add the capers. Slice the veal very thin and place in a glass or pottery (not metal) bowl. Pour the sauce over it and let marinate in the refrigerator for 12 hours. Serve with sliced tomatoes.

| | |
|---|---|
| *Brandied Pâté* | 2 cans Sell's liver pâté<br>2 small cans mushroom bits and pieces<br>1 loaf icebox rye<br>½ stick butter (⅛ pound)<br>¼ cup best brandy |

Melt butter over medium heat in frying pan. Drain thoroughly contents of 2 small cans mushroom bits and sauté in butter until well browned. Add 2 cans Sell's liver pâté and ¼ cup good brandy. Stir thoroughly and refrigerate until needed. Serve with slices of icebox rye bread.

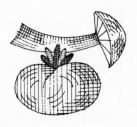

Soups

### Onion Soup au Gratin

4 or 5 Spanish onions, peeled and sliced or diced
4 tablespoons butter
1 quart stock or chicken broth, or 4 or 5 chicken or beef bouillon cubes dissolved in 1 quart water
Salt and pepper
Toasted French bread
Grated Parmesan cheese

Sauté onions in butter until lightly browned. Add stock, broth, or bouillon either to the skillet in which you have browned the onions or to a large casserole to which you transfer the onions. Salt and pepper to taste, allow the soup to come to a boil, and simmer 15 minutes. Serve with slices of well-toasted French bread heaped with grated Parmesan cheese and lightly browned under the broiler. Serve with additional grated cheese.

### VARIATIONS

### Clear Onion Soup

Strain soup. Serve with toasted French bread and grated Parmesan cheese.

### Onion Soup with Wine

Add ½ cup dry white wine to the broth after adding broth to the onions.

## Onion Soup
## in Casserole

Transfer soup to individual casseroles. Top each one with a slice of toast and heap with grated cheese. Place in a moderate oven (375°) for 10 minutes.

## Chicken and
## Onion Soup

With a salad and hot French bread, this makes a perfect party soup. Cook a large fat chicken as you would for ordinary chicken soup. When the chicken is just about tender, strain, cool the broth and skim off the fat. In this fat, fry at least 4 or 5 thin-sliced onions. Don't let them burn but cook them slowly until they are mushy and transparent. Bone the chicken, leaving the meat in large pieces. Reduce the broth somewhat; this soup should be almost as thick as a stew. Add the chicken pieces and onions to the broth, season well, add a little chopped celery and some whole mushrooms and simmer only until these are tender. Thicken the soup lightly with cornstarch mixed with water; pour this elegant concoction into a large tureen over toasted pieces of French bread sprinkled with grated Parmesan cheese.

21

## Green Vichyssoise

[SERVES 4]

1 can potato soup
1 can chicken broth or consommé
1 soup-can water
1 cucumber

Dice cucumber but *do not peel*. Put in blender for 10 seconds at medium speed. Adjust blender to low speed and add soups and water. Mix for 2 or 3 seconds more. Garnish with finely chopped chives or parsley. If all ingredients are thoroughly chilled beforehand, this may be served at once.

## Jellied Borscht

[SERVES 4]

1 can tomato soup
1 can beef consommé
1 can water
1 can strained beets (for babies)
1 small white onion, finely chopped
2 tablespoons lemon juice
½ teaspoon sugar
1 envelope gelatin

Partially dissolve gelatin, at least until soft, in ½ soup-can of water. Mix in top of double boiler all other ingredients and heat through. Add gelatin and stir until completely dissolved. Remove from heat, cool and refrigerate until jellied. Garnish each portion with heaping teaspoon of sour cream seasoned with mixed herbs.

*Cioppino*

[SERVES 6]

½ cup olive oil
¼ cup parsley
1 #2 can solid-pack tomatoes
2 cans tomato purée
Salt, pepper
1 pound fillet of fish
1 large or 2 small lobsters
1 tablespoon minced garlic
1 stalk celery
½ green pepper, minced
2 cups red wine
½ teaspoon basil
24 clams in shell
2 pounds shrimp

Have lobster cut in serving pieces while raw. Shell shrimp, wash clams under cold water, scrubbing thoroughly. Cut fish fillets in 2-inch pieces.

Make sauce by putting ½ cup olive oil in large, heavy casserole. Sauté minced parsley, garlic, celery and green pepper until limp, then add tomatoes and tomato purée. Add 2 cups dry red wine, dash of salt and pepper and ½ teaspoon dried basil. Simmer gently one hour.

Meanwhile, steam clams in very little water until opened. Set clams in shell aside, strain broth left into sauce. Fifteen minutes before serving, add fish fillets, shrimp and lobster. Just before serving, add clams. (A meal in itself—serve with plenty of crusty French or Italian bread, in chunks, without butter, for dunking up the Cioppino sauce.)

23

### Crab-Meat Bisque

[SERVES 4]

10½-ounce can each of concentrated tomato soup and pea soup
6½-ounce can crab meat
1 cup cream
¾ cup sherry

Clean the crab meat. Place soups and cream in a saucepan and heat, stirring constantly. Add crab meat, heat thoroughly. Just before serving add sherry gradually. Serve hot with crackers.

### European Summer Soup (Gazpacho)

This is a surprisingly good cold soup, and hardly known in this country. A strong beef broth is needed, chilled and every speck of fat skimmed off, or undiluted canned consommé may be used. No further cooking is required, and the vegetables used must be absolutely fresh. Crush a clove of garlic in a large bowl, remove it, and now add whatever fresh delights your garden offers, all very finely cubed or shredded. There must be at least ½ cup chopped raw vegetables for each cup of broth, and among these there must be peeled cucumbers, a good supply of scallions and a green pepper, each cut very small, and ripe, ruddy tomatoes, skinned, the seeds squeezed out, and the pulp diced. Dribble over 1½ teaspoons real olive oil and ½ teaspoon lemon juice for each cup of broth, season with salt, fresh pepper and a dusting of sugar, and add the broth. A sweet red pepper is also good in this; so is spinach cut into minute ribbons, small whole black olives, or any of the salad herbs such as tarragon, chervil, parsley, basil or, best of all, fresh dill. Serve ice-cold in ice-cold cups. One taste on a hot day is like leaping into a cold stream. Afterward, a lazy nap.

25

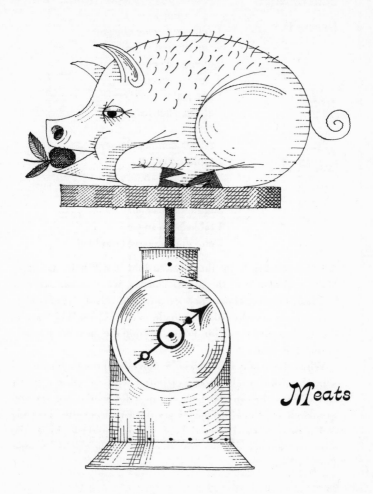

*Meats*

## *Sauerbraten*

[SERVES 4]

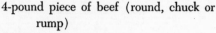

4-pound piece of beef (round, chuck or rump)
1½ cups red wine vinegar
½ cup dry red wine
2 onions, sliced
2 carrots, sliced
1 bay leaf
3 allspice berries
3 cloves
1 tablespoon peppercorns
1 tablespoon salt
8 tablespoons butter
1 tablespoon oil
5 tablespoons flour
1 tablespoon sugar
⅔ cup gingersnaps, crumbled

Ask the butcher to tie the meat so that it will hold its shape. Make a marinade of the mixed vinegar, wine, onions, carrots, bay leaf, allspice, cloves, peppercorns and salt. Put the beef in a deep bowl and pour the marinade over it. Cover and leave in the refrigerator to soak for 3 days, turning the meat occasionally during this time.

When the beef is well soaked, remove from the marinade and wipe dry. Melt 4 tablespoons of butter with the oil in a heavy Dutch oven. Brown the beef on all sides in the hot fat and sprinkle it lightly with flour as you turn it. Heat the marinade and pour over the browned beef. Cover the kettle, lower the heat and simmer gently until the beef is thoroughly tender, about 3 hours.

When the meat is done, pour off the sauce and set the kettle on one side to keep the meat warm. Skim fat from sauce and strain it. In a heavy skillet, melt 4 tablespoons butter and blend in 4 tablespoons flour and the sugar. Cook gently until flour and sugar are slightly browned. Add the strained sauce slowly, stirring it until it is smooth and thickened. Add the gingersnaps to the sauce. Pour over the meat, cover and cook gently for ½ hour. The traditional accompaniment for sauerbraten is dumplings, but we prefer noodles.

### Ground Beef in Cabbage Leaves

[SERVES 4]

1 pound lean raw beef, ground
Salt and pepper to taste
1 small onion
½ cup cooked rice
2 cups tomatoes
1 onion, chopped
2 tablespoons vinegar
2 tablespoons sugar
8 large leaves of cabbage

Pour boiling water over the cabbage leaves to make them less brittle. Season the meat with salt and pepper, add grated onion and rice. Roll a portion of the meat mixture in each leaf. Fasten with toothpicks. Place them in a kettle with the rest of the ingredients, add a little water and simmer until cabbage is tender and well browned. The sauce may be thickened with crumbled gingersnaps.

## Beef Collops Flambés

[SERVES 4]

2 pounds top sirloin, cut into 2-inch cubes
2 onions, sliced paper thin
1 cup red wine
2 tablespoons tarragon vinegar
½ cup olive oil
2 teaspoons salt
½ teaspoon pepper
¼ teaspoon marjoram, rosemary or
    oregano
Whole mushroom crowns
Green pepper slices
Small whole tomatoes
½ cup brandy

Marinate the meat overnight in the onion-wine-vinegar-oil-herb-salt-pepper mixture. When ready to roast, alternate pieces of meat on spit with mushroom crowns, green pepper slices and tomatoes. Roast about 15 minutes, basting frequently. When ready to serve, warm brandy, ignite, pour over meat, and serve flambé.

### VARIATIONS

2-inch cubes of beef, rolled in bacon, and alternated on spit with tomato slices and canned onions. Roast about 15 minutes, basting with sherry and Worcestershire sauce.

2-inch cubes of beef, marinated in soy sauce, alternated on spit with chicken livers. Roast for 15 minutes, basting with the marinade to which a little vermouth is added.

*Marinated*
*Steak*
*(outdoors)*

⅔ cup olive oil
½ teaspoon fresh-ground pepper
Dash of salt
Juice of 1 lemon
1 clove garlic

One of the most delicious steaks I have ever eaten was marinated in olive oil and condiments for 12 hours before it was broiled. Try it this way:

Mix olive oil with pepper, salt and lemon juice. If you like the flavor of garlic with steak, rub the meat lightly with a clove of garlic before placing it in the oil. Let the steak stand in this marinade in a warm place 12 or 15 hours, or even 24 hours. Turn it several times. When ready to broil, remove the steak from the oil and grill as usual. Be economical—use some of the same oil to grill onions to be served with the steak.

## *Beef Goulash with Red Cabbage*

[SERVES 6]

Brown darkly 3 pounds of cubed beef stew meat in hot fat along with 2 sliced onions. Cover with water, and add salt and pepper, 1 teaspoon caraway seed and a bay leaf. Simmer slowly. About half an hour before tender, sprinkle over 3 table-spoons tarragon or wine vinegar or ½ cup dry red wine, and cover with a medium red cabbage cut into eighths. When the cabbage of this excellent dish is done, thicken the gravy with gingersnaps to taste.

31

## Leftover Rare Beef with Sauce

Have the meat at room temperature, slice it thin and place on a warmed platter. Have ready a sauce made by browning ¼ pound finely sliced mushrooms in 3 tablespoons butter, to which you have added ½ cup water, ¼ cup red wine, 1 bouillon cube, 1 teaspoon tomato paste, 1 teaspoon Kitchen Bouquet and a dash of Worcestershire. Thicken with cornstarch and pour over the meat.

## Rollatini

[SERVES 8]

¼ cup olive oil
⅛ pound butter
Garlic
4 tablespoons chopped parsley
4 tablespoons chopped chives or scallions
16 pieces veal, 4″ x 6″
2 Mozzarella cheeses or ½ pound
　　Gruyère
8 slices boiled ham or prosciutto ham
1 cup white wine
½ pound fresh mushrooms
Pepper
Flour

Brown a clove of garlic in butter and olive oil in large casserole. Remove garlic and discard. Lay thin veal slices flat, cover with slice of ham and slice of cheese. (Prosciutto ham is hard to find; boiled ham is an adequate substitute.) Season with pepper, sprinkle with mixture of chopped chives or scallion tops and parsley. Roll up and fasten with toothpicks. Dust rolls with flour. Brown in garlic-flavored oil-butter. Add mushrooms, sliced, and cook, covered, for ½ hour, then add white wine and continue to cook approximately 1 more hour, until sauce is thick and veal tender.

## Veal Chops
## Anne de Beaujeu

Allow 1 chop per serving. Dip the chops in flour, then in beaten egg and again in flour. Sauté them in butter until well browned on both sides and tender. Season to taste and arrange them in a shallow ovenproof pottery or metal baking dish. Top the chops with the following sauce, which has been made in advance:

For 4 servings, finely chop 1½ cups of onion. Mix with 6 tablespoons of butter in a skillet and put over low heat. Cover the pan and let the onions steam in the butter until soft and juicy. Pour off 3 tablespoons of the butter-onion liquid and blend with 3 tablespoons of flour and cook this roux until well thickened. Place the rest of the onion-butter mixture in an electric blender and blend for 1 minute, or force it through a fine sieve. Mix with the flour and onion juice and cook over a medium flame until blended and thickened. Add ⅔ cup of cream and ⅔ cup of grated Gruyère or Switzerland Swiss cheese and stir until the cheese is melted and mixed into the sauce. Add salt and pepper to taste and a dash of nutmeg.

Pour this sauce over the chops and sprinkle with a little more grated cheese. Put the baking dish in a very hot oven or under the broiler flame to melt the cheese and heat through.

33

## *Ossi Bucchi*

Shank bones of veal
Rice
Veal broth or chicken broth
Saffron
Flour
3 or 4 tomatoes
Parsley
Olive oil
1 cup water
½ cup white wine
1 clove garlic
½ teaspoon basil
2 medium-sized onions

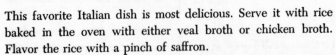

This favorite Italian dish is most delicious. Serve it with rice baked in the oven with either veal broth or chicken broth. Flavor the rice with a pinch of saffron.

Have the butcher cut veal shank into serving pieces 3 inches long. Use one piece for each serving. Dredge the pieces in flour and sear in hot olive oil until nicely browned. Add water and white wine and bring to a boil. Cover and simmer for 20 minutes.

Add garlic, basil, tomatoes (peeled, seeded and cut in small pieces), onions (finely chopped), and a sprig of parsley. Continue simmering until tender—1½ to 2 hours.

Remove the meat to a hot dish or casserole and allow the sauce to reduce by cooking it uncovered for 5 minutes. If you wish a thicker sauce, knead together butter and flour and drop into the sauce, stirring the while. Correct seasoning and pour sauce over meat.

## *Sweetbreads en Brochette*

[SERVES 4–6]

2 pairs sweetbreads
18 to 20 mushrooms
4 or 5 rashers bacon
Butter
Salt and pepper
Chopped parsley

Cut prepared sweetbreads in 1-inch squares. Wash and remove stems from mushrooms. Cut bacon in 1-inch pieces and sauté for a few minutes until partially cooked. Drain on absorbent paper.

Alternate pieces of sweetbread, mushroom caps, and squares of bacon on medium-sized skewers, allowing one skewer for each serving. Brush well with butter, sprinkle with salt and pepper, and broil, turning frequently until the sweetbreads are nicely browned and the mushrooms cooked. Sprinkle with chopped parsley and pour a little melted butter over each skewer before serving.

### VARIATIONS

You may use small cubes of ham with the sweetbreads, or use the tiny plum or cherry tomatoes for a change of flavor.

## Kebabs
## or
## Shashlik

[SERVES 6]

2 to 2½ pounds lamb
½ cup olive oil
1 cup red wine
3 tablespoons wine vinegar
Thyme
1 teaspoon salt
1 bay leaf
2 cloves garlic, crushed
Parsley, chopped
Oregano

From Persia to New York there are many different combinations of lamb and accompaniments that take their place on skewers, brochettes, sticks, or imitation swords and are broiled over charcoal or under gas or electricity. Lamb thus cooked is nearly always marinated.

The meat should be cut in squares or cubes 1 to 2 inches square. You may use wire or steel skewers; the size varies according to the type. I suggest fairly substantial ones about 9 or 10 inches long.

For the marinade, mix salt, olive oil, red wine, wine vinegar, bay leaf crushed into small pieces, garlic, parsley, thyme, and a little oregano.

Soak the lamb in the marinade for several hours; the longer the better. If you are planning the dish for evening, prepare the marinade first thing in the morning and allow the lamb to soak all day.

Arrange the squares of seasoned lamb on the skewers. Alternate the lamb with bacon or salt-pork squares and with tiny onions or tomatoes if you wish.

Broil quickly under a brisk flame or over hot coals. Turn frequently so that the meat becomes evenly cooked. You may for variety use mushrooms, kidneys, or other seasonings with the lamb.

Serve at once with baked rice.

*Scaloppine with Mushrooms and White Wine*

[SERVES 4]

2 pounds veal, in thin scallops
Flour
Salt
Black pepper
Paprika
4 tablespoons butter
3 or 4 shallots or small white onions
1 cup mushrooms, sliced
½ cup white wine
1 tablespoon parsley, chopped
Few leaves tarragon

Dredge scallops with flour seasoned with salt, freshly ground black pepper, and paprika. Sauté the scallops slowly in the butter, and when they are nicely browned place them in a hot casserole or pan to keep warm.

When all the scallops are cooked, add to the butter in the pan the shallots or onions, finely chopped, and sauté for 2 minutes. Add sliced mushrooms and blend well with the onion or shallots. Add ¼ cup white wine and allow it to cook down for a few minutes.

Add parsley and tarragon.

Finally, add another ¼ cup white wine and allow all to boil up for 1 or 2 minutes before pouring over the scallops.

## Sugared Leg
## of Spring Lamb

Salt and pepper a young leg of lamb, spread it generously with wet mustard and pack it with dark brown sugar as you would a ham for baking. Place uncovered in a preheated 325° oven and watch that the sugar does not scorch on the bottom of the roaster. Baste often with the sharp-sweet juices and if the sugar begins to burn, add a small amount of black coffee. At any rate, when the lamb is about half done, pour over a cup of strong black coffee, left over from breakfast or lunch. Roast until the meat is tender but not dry; about 2 hours should be long enough. Thicken the gravy with cornstarch and melt into it 1 good teaspoon of currant jelly. Let the sauce simmer 5 minutes, adding more water if needed.

## Roast Marinated
## Leg of Lamb

Marinate the lamb for 24 hours before cooking. Use plenty of herbs, for lamb is exceedingly friendly to all sorts of herb flavoring. For a leg of lamb use ½ cup olive oil, 2 teaspoons salt, 1 teaspoon black pepper, the juice of 2 lemons, 1 clove garlic, a healthy infusion of thyme, parsley, and oregano, and onions and a bay leaf. Add to this a pint of wine, either red or white, and allow the roast to absorb all the goodness of the mixture. Turn several times during the marinating period.

There are two schools of thought on roasting marinated lamb. Some say it should be roasted in the marinade in a slow oven

(300°), and basted with the marinade while cooking. Others insist it should be cooked in a very hot oven without basting. In either case, I believe that the results are about the same, and they are exceedingly good. Allow the same roasting time and meat temperatures as for plain roast lamb.

You may treat the boned shoulder roast the same way as a leg of lamb.

Serve lamb on a hot platter and on hot plates. Nothing is more unappetizing than a slice of lamb on a cold plate with congealed fat. Serve the juices from the pan over the roast.

## Chops
## Charcutière

This is a classic way of serving pork chops in France. Sauté 8 chops in pork fat. When they are browned and have simmered for a few minutes add 2 large onions, finely chopped. Cover the pan and let the onions cook down with the meat. Uncover and salt and pepper to taste. When the chops are done remove them to a hot platter. Add 1½ cups bouillon (or boiling water and a bouillon cube) to the pan and bring it to a boil. Add ½ cup tomato purée, 1 teaspoon dry mustard and ½ teaspoon freshly ground black pepper. Thicken the sauce lightly with *beurre manié* (butter and flour kneaded together into small balls). Just before serving add 2 tablespoons or more of finely chopped sour gherkins and sprinkle with chopped parsley. Arrange the chops around a mound of creamy mashed potatoes and serve the sauce separately.

## Favorite Spareribs

[ONE POUND PER SERVING]

Chop 4 cloves garlic very fine and mix with the juice of 4 lemons, ¼ cup soy sauce, ½ cup honey, 2 teaspoons basil, 1½ teaspoons freshly ground black pepper and ¼ cup chopped parsley. Put two sides of spareribs in this mixture and let them stand for 2 hours, turning them frequently. Wind the ribs on spits or put them on a rack in a roasting pan. Grill over medium heat or cook in a 350° oven for about 1 hour. Brush occasionally with a mixture of honey and lemon juice. The ribs should be nicely glazed when done.

Serve with fried rice and broiled onion slices or thinly sliced beefsteak tomatoes and thinly sliced onion with basil dressing.

## Spanish Stuffed Roast Pork

[SERVES 6]

4-5 pounds loin of pork roast
¼ cup olive oil
½ green pepper, chopped
1 onion, chopped
Clove garlic, crushed
2 cans tomato sauce
¼ cup sherry
1½ tablespoons chili powder
1 cup chopped ripe olives
½ cup raisins
2 cups cooked rice
1 can consommé

Have the butcher split the roast so that a stuffing can be placed inside it. Make a sauce as follows: Sauté green pepper, onion and garlic in olive oil until tender. Add salt and pepper, 2 cans of tomato sauce and the can of consommé, undiluted. Let simmer a bit, then add sherry and chili powder and simmer a few minutes more. Add chopped olives and raisins at the last and simmer 5 more minutes. Add ¾ cup of this sauce to the cooked rice, and stuff the roast. Roast approximately 2 hours in medium oven. At the end of the first hour, remove from the oven, take off any excess fat, and spoon any remaining sauce and rice over and around. Return to oven for final hour.

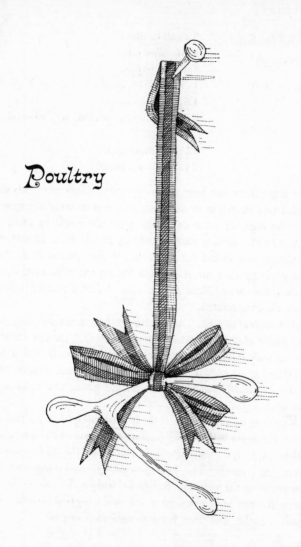

*Poultry*

### Chicken Sauté Marengo

[SERVES 4–6]

2 small broilers
¼ cup olive oil
Salt and pepper
1 clove garlic, crushed
1 jigger cognac
½ cup tomatoes, peeled, seeded, and cut fine
12 mushroom caps
2 tablespoons butter

*For years there has been a gastronomical battle over this dish, which had its origin in necessity of the most exacting type. It was the night of June 14, 1800, after the battle of Marengo. It had been a victory marred only by the death of Desaix, and Napoleon had called his generals together and ordered food. The generals were far away from the source of provisions, and Dunan, the chef of Napoleon, was faced with providing a dinner from absolute scratch.*

*A resourceful man, Dunan inquired at a neighboring farm and found that he could acquire chickens. A garden close by offered only tomatoes and garlic. Dunan himself had a flask of oil and some cognac. He cleaned the chickens, sautéed them in the oil, added the tomatoes and the garlic, and swilled the pan with cognac.*

*Napoleon and the generals must have enjoyed it, for the dish has come down to our time, bearing the name of the battle site. Other chefs have added many things to the dish—crawfish, fried eggs, mushrooms, and practically everything else—and claimed it is the original. But to be truly a disciple of Dunan you will sauté your chickens in oil, add chopped tomatoes and crushed garlic, and rinse the pan well with cognac.*

Prepare broilers for sauté. Heat olive oil in a skillet and brown the pieces of chicken on both sides. Salt and pepper well, reduce the flame, and continue cooking. When the chicken is half cooked, after about 10 minutes, add garlic. When the chicken is tender, remove it to a hot platter and keep warm.

Add to the pan the tomatoes and 1 jigger cognac. Allow the tomatoes to cook down in the oil and cognac for 4 or 5 minutes or until the sauce is well blended. Serve with a garnish of sautéed mushroom caps, prepared by sautéing the caps in 2 tablespoons butter for 10 minutes, or until tender. Salt and pepper to taste, and serve with the chicken.

## Smothered Chicken

Here is a delicious favorite method of preparing larger fowl. Cut a chicken into pieces (or use frozen breasts and thighs) and shake them in a paper bag with a mixture of pepper, salt and flour. Be sure the pieces are well coated. Brown them in a skillet in butter or chicken fat and arrange in a large casserole. Douse with paprika. Then pour over ¾ cup dry vermouth, ¾ cup cream, the juices from the frying pan, and enough milk almost to cover the chicken. Bake in a 375° oven uncovered, turning often and stirring up the sauce. The chicken should be very tender, almost leaving the bone, and the sauce thick and curdlike. It is delicious to serve over rice, either plain or fried in butter with a little onion and herbs.

45

### Chicken Breasts with Tomato and Wine Sauce

[SERVES 6]

3 whole chicken breasts
3 tablespoons butter
2 tablespoons olive oil
1 medium-sized onion, finely chopped
4 tablespoons flour
1½ cups chicken stock
¾ cup thick tomato juice
Salt, pepper
¼ cup sherry (dry)
2 tablespoons chopped parsley

Skin and bone the breasts and cut them in half. Brown them slowly on both sides in the hot butter and oil. Remove them from the pan. Lightly brown the chopped onion in the same pan. Blend in the flour, then pour on the stock and tomato juice. Stir until the mixture comes to a boil, and season with salt and pepper. Add the chicken, sherry and parsley. Simmer covered until the chicken is tender, about 30-40 minutes.

### Buttermilk-Fried Chicken and Biscuits

Cut a frying chicken into serving pieces, reserving the back, wings and giblets. Soak the chicken for half an hour in 1½ cups creamy buttermilk. Meanwhile make a rich broth from the back, wings, giblets and a stalk of celery. This will be used in making the biscuits.

To fry the chicken, remove the pieces from the buttermilk but do not dry them. Shake the pieces into a bag containing flour, salt, pepper and 1 tablespoon minced parsley. Then brown them in chicken fat or in hot oil and butter until golden. Pour the remaining buttermilk in a baking dish and add the browned chicken. Bake uncovered in a 250° oven until tender, about 1½ or 2 hours. The chicken should be deliciously crisp, and a good gravy for the biscuits may be made by adding milk to the drippings, thickening with flour if necessary.

For the biscuits, use any good baking-powder dough. Reduce the broth until fully flavored (there should be at least a good cupful, however), thicken very lightly with cornstarch, add 1 tablespoon minced parsley and pour this into an oblong biscuit pan. Cut the biscuits ¾ inch thick and place them next to each other right in the broth. Bake biscuits as usual.

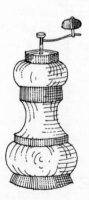

### Duck with Orange

[SERVES 4]

1 5-6 pound duck
Salt, pepper
2 large oranges
1 small onion
2 teaspoons potato flour
1½ cups orange juice
½ cup red wine
1 tablespoon red currant jelly

Season the duck lightly. Stuff with one orange, quartered, and the onion, and tie the legs together. Roast in a moderate (350°) oven breast side up for 2-2¼ hours. Keep pouring off the fat so that when the duck is cooked there are only about 2-3 tablespoons fat in the pan with the brown glaze. Meanwhile, cut thin slices of the peel from the other orange with a vegetable peeler and cut them in julienne strips. Cover with cold water, bring to a boil and drain. Section the orange. Remove stuffing from the duck, place the duck on a hot serving platter and keep warm. Blend the potato flour into the pan juices. Pour on the orange juice and red wine and stir until the sauce comes to a boil. Add the currant jelly and orange rind and taste for seasoning. Simmer for a few minutes. Just before serving add the orange sections. Spoon a little of the sauce over the duck and serve the rest separately.

VARIATION

### Duck with Cherries

Follow the preceding recipe but substitute 1 cup of sour red cherries for the orange sections, cherry juice for the orange juice (or use half and half), and add a little kirsch to the red wine.

### Barbecued Herb Chicken (outdoors)

[SERVES 6]

3 halved broiler chickens
¼ pound butter
1 cup white wine (dry, not sweet)
½ cup salad oil
¼ cup Chinese soy sauce
1 tablespoon minced parsley
½ teaspoon marjoram
¼ teaspoon tarragon
1 garlic clove
¼ teaspoon salt

Make a mixture of the ¼ pound of butter, the tablespoon of minced parsley, the ¼ teaspoon of tarragon, and the ½ teaspoon of marjoram. Using a dull knife, lift the skin from the breast meat of the halved chickens, and insert the blend of butter and seasoning. Spread the blend around under the skin as widely as possible, making sure the skin is not so detached it will come off when the chicken is turned on the grill.

Make a marinade of the salad oil, wine, soy sauce, the crushed garlic clove, and salt. Let chicken stand in marinade overnight, or for several hours at least, and turn chicken once during this period.

Grill the chicken halves breast down over glowing coals on a greased rack. Turn halves occasionally while basting with marinade until golden brown—which should take ½ hour.

49

## *Turkey Leftovers in White Wine Sauce*

Cut the leftover turkey, preferably the breast, into neat, thin slices. Lay these generously over pieces of good crisp toast in a flat baking dish or individual casseroles. Sprinkle over some halved mushrooms, previously browned in butter. Now pour over a good amount of cream sauce, seasoned with a little rosemary, and to which you have added dry white wine or sherry to taste. Shake enough grated Parmesan cheese over the top to make a nice coating, add a few slivered almonds if you like and some chopped parsley, dot well with butter, and put in a hot oven for a few minutes, just long enough to heat.

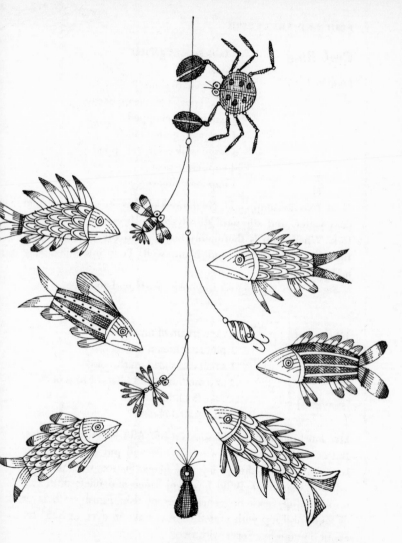

Fish and Shellfish

### Crab Ring

[SERVES 6]

2 tablespoons gelatin
½ cup water
1 can tomato soup
3 small packages cream cheese
1 cucumber, chopped
1 teaspoon grated onion
1 large stalk celery, chopped
4 cups crab meat
1 cup mayonnaise

Heat tomato soup, add gelatin which has been softened in cold water, and stir until dissolved. Mash cream cheese with fork. When soup is thoroughly cooled, add the vegetables, all the other ingredients, and blend well. Pour into oiled ring mold. Chill.

Serve with asparagus, artichoke hearts and tomatoes.

### Fish and Mushroom Casserole

[SERVES 4]

2 cans cream of mushroom soup
1 pint sour cream
1 small can sliced mushrooms
4 or 5 medium-sized fillets of bass or
    flounder
¼ cup grated cheese

Mix mushroom soup and sour cream. Add sliced mushrooms. Butter a heavy earthenware casserole and put a layer of this sauce in bottom; then a layer of fillets. Season with pinch of salt and marjoram. Build layers of sauce and fillets until casserole is full, seasoning each layer of fish. Finish with layer of sauce and top with grated cheese. Bake in oven at 325° for about 35 minutes. Serve with rice.

## Fillets Florentine

[SERVES 4]

2 pounds spinach
Salt
4 tablespoons butter
½ cup water
½ cup white wine
3 peppercorns
1 small onion stuck with 1 clove
Sprig of parsley
4 fish fillets
2 tablespoons flour
¼ cup heavy cream
Few grains nutmeg
Few drops lemon juice
Grated Parmesan cheese

Cook the spinach, drain, and chop very fine. Season to taste with salt and add 2 tablespoons butter. Arrange the spinach on a well-buttered oval baking dish and keep warm.

Combine water with white wine, peppercorns, onion, and parsley. Bring to a boil and let cook 5 minutes. Add fish fillets (1 to a person) and simmer for 5 minutes or until fish is just cooked through. Remove to a hot plate, let the liquor simmer 2 or 3 minutes longer and strain. Melt 2 tablespoons butter in a saucepan or in upper part of double boiler and blend it well with flour. Stirring constantly, gradually add the strained broth from the fish; continue stirring until thickened. Add cream, correct seasoning, and add nutmeg and lemon juice.

Place cooked fillets on the bed of spinach, cover with the sauce, and sprinkle liberally with grated Parmesan cheese. Place the dish in a very hot oven (475°) for 5 minutes or until the cheese is delicately browned.

53

## Stuffed Fillets

[SERVES 4]

9 tablespoons butter
1 teaspoon scraped onion
6 finely chopped mushrooms
12 mushroom caps
1 tablespoon chopped parsley
½ cup crab meat
Salt
4 fish fillets
¾ cup white wine
½ cup water
3 peppercorns
3 or 4 sprigs parsley
Thyme
2 tablespoons flour
¼ cup heavy cream
2 egg yolks
Buttered crumbs
Grated Parmesan cheese

Select thin and broad fillets. Lemon sole and gray sole (flounder) are the best.

Melt 3 tablespoons butter in a small skillet. Sauté for 3 minutes the onion, mushrooms, and parsley, and combine with crab meat. Salt to taste and blend well. Reserving the mushroom caps, spread this mixture on fish fillets, and roll and secure with toothpick or tie with light string.

Combine white wine with water, ¼ teaspoon salt, peppercorns, parsley, and a little thyme, and bring to the boiling point. Simmer rolled fillets in bouillon 6 to 8 minutes, basting frequently. When fish is cooked, remove carefully to a shallow baking dish. Strain the broth and reserve it.

In the upper part of the double boiler combine 2 tablespoons butter and the flour, and blend well. Add, stirring constantly, 1 cup strained broth, and continue stirring until nicely thickened. Blend in heavy cream mixed with egg yolks and stir until well blended; do not let it boil. Pour the sauce over the fillets, from which you have removed the toothpicks or string. Sprinkle with buttered crumbs and grated Parmesan cheese and place under the broiler for just a minute to brown lightly. Garnish with sautéed mushroom caps and serve at once.

## *Poached Salmon*

[SERVES 6–8]

3-4 pound piece of salmon, center cut
1 cup dry white wine
1 carrot
1 onion
2-3 cloves
6 peppercorns
1 bay leaf
1 stalk celery
1 tablespoon salt
¼ cup parsley
Cheesecloth

In a pan large enough to hold the fish, put 2 quarts water, the white wine, the vegetables, coarsely chopped, the seasonings. Bring to a boil and let cook 5 to 10 minutes. (Fish bones and trimmings can be added for additional flavor.)

Wrap salmon in cheesecloth and place in simmering court bouillon, turning fire as low as possible. Cook 10 minutes for each pound of fish, until salmon flakes easily with a fork. Remove cooked salmon and serve either hot or cold.

## Lobster Américaine

[SERVES 2]

The lobster must be alive. Cut the tail into slices; remove all the legs; break the claws to facilitate removal of the meat after cooking; cut the body of the lobster in two lengthwise; remove the sac found at the top of the head, which usually contains gravel. Save the intestines and the coral; season the pieces of tail meat with salt and pepper.

To prepare a lobster weighing about 1 pound: Heat 4 tablespoons oil and 1 ounce butter until very hot in a deep frying pan; drop in the pieces of lobster; sauté them until the flesh becomes firm and the shell turns bright red. Holding the lid tightly on the pan, pour off the fat; sprinkle 2 chopped shallots and a crushed clove of garlic onto the lobster pieces; add 1 small glass of flaming cognac, 6 ounces white wine, 4 ounces fish stock, 1 tablespoon melted meat glaze, 3 pressed, peeled, chopped tomatoes or 1½ tablespoons tomato purée, 1 pinch crushed parsley, and a dash of cayenne. Cover the pan and cook in the oven 15-20 minutes. Remove the lobster pieces and place them on a platter; remove the shell from the slices of lobster meat and the meat from the claws and place them in a timbale; arrange the half shells of the lobster on top so that they lean on each other and stand up. Keep hot. Reduce the cooking sauce to 6 ounces; add the chopped intestines with ½ tablespoon butter; cook for a few moments, and strain. Heat again without boiling, remove from the fire, and finish with 4 ounces butter divided into small pieces; pour over the lobster pieces and sprinkle with a pinch of crushed parsley.

## *Coulibiac*

[SERVES 6]

Brioche dough
3 hard-cooked eggs, chopped
½ pint sour cream
1 pound smoked salmon, thinly sliced
¾ pound cooked shrimp
Fresh chopped dill
Beaten egg yolk

To make brioche dough, put 1½ cups flour in a bowl and add 3 large beaten eggs, 2 teaspoons sugar and ½ teaspoon salt. Work to a dough and beat on a board until light. Mix in 5 ounces creamed butter and 1 package yeast that has been dissolved in ¼ cup warm water. Mix in ½ cup more flour and let stand until dough rises. Place in a lightly greased and floured bowl, cover with a cloth, and allow to rise until double its bulk at room temperature. Chill overnight in the refrigerator (or for 1 hour in the deep-freeze). Remove, roll out to ½-inch thickness on a floured board, brush with melted butter and sprinkle with a few browned bread crumbs.

Put a layer of finely chopped egg on top of the dough and dot with sour cream. On top of this put thin slices of salmon and thin slices of shrimp and sprinkle with dill. Dot with more sour cream and roll up like a jelly roll. Put in a well greased bread tin, cover with a cloth and put to rise in a warm place for ¼ hour. Brush with beaten egg yolk and bake in a 425° oven for 30 minutes. Remove, turn out, and serve.

## Special Broiled Shrimp (India)

[SERVES 4]

2 pounds shrimp
1 cup oil
1½ teaspoons chili powder mixed with
    1 tablespoon vinegar
¼ teaspoon black pepper
3 cloves garlic, minced
1 teaspoon salt
1 tablespoon basil
1 tablespoon chopped mint leaves

Wash, shell and dry the shrimp. Make a marinade of the oil, spices, garlic, salt and herbs. Mix well, pour over shrimp and leave to marinate overnight or at least for 4 hours. Place the shrimp with the marinade in a broiling pan. Under a high flame, broil the shrimp for 6 to 10 minutes (depending on their size). Turn them once while broiling and serve with as much marinade as you prefer.

## Scallops

The delicate tiny bay scallops are so delicious by themselves and so easily overwhelmed by elaborate sauces that the best way to prepare them is a simple sauté. Wash them and dry them and sprinkle just very lightly with flour. Heat half olive oil and half butter and add the scallops, tossing them about to brown a bit. They will only need a minute or two. Season with salt and pepper while they cook and add a sprinkling of chopped parsley and a pinch or so of tarragon, if you like. At the very last minute, add a dash or two of lemon juice and a bit of dry white wine. Do not overcook the scallops. They should be tender and juicy. As with oysters, the amount per serving depends on the size of the scallops.

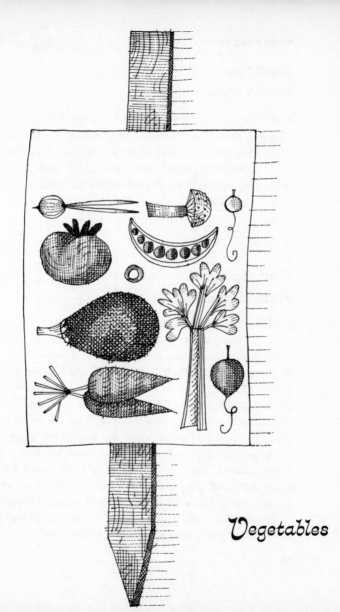

*Vegetables*

## Small Peas, French Style

Place the peas in a stewpan with a good handful of finely chopped lettuce, a few small new onions, a piece of butter; add a little salt, a pinch of sugar, a small bunch of chervil; half cover with boiling water, and cook slowly with the pan covered. The cooking time depends upon the quality of the peas and the quantity of water.

## Cauliflower and Fresh Mushrooms

Cauliflower, like cabbage, is usually ruined by overcooking. Take a young snowy head, leaving on some of the delicate inside leaves, and steam it whole in salted water reaching only to the top of the stalk—¼ inch deep should be enough. Cook it only until it can be pierced lightly with a fork. Drain and keep dry on a platter in a warm oven. (Don't ever keep drained vegetables warm in a covered pot because the steam will only draw off more juices and make the vegetables soggy.) Meanwhile prepare ½ pound whole mushrooms by frying them in butter, covered for 3 or 4 minutes and uncovered for 3 or 4 more. Salt and pepper them, sprinkle with a few drops of lemon juice and minced parsley, heap them around the head of cauliflower; over all, pour a cup of cream sauce in which you have melted just a little Swiss or Cheddar cheese.

## Water Chestnut Casserole

Cut a bunch of Pascal celery into 1-inch pieces. Cook in a large 14-ounce can of chicken broth (or in homemade broth if you have it, of course) until it is nearly tender. Be careful not to let it get soft. Thicken the broth with 2 tablespoons cornstarch, season, pour it and the celery into a casserole and add 1 can water chestnuts, sliced, and ¼ cup blanched, slivered almonds. Sprinkle with bread crumbs, dot with butter, and bake ½ hour in a moderate oven. You'll find this unusual dish, with its crunchy surprises, perfect to serve with cold fowl or a cold roast.

## Carrots and Fresh Mint

Slice young lean carrots into thin 2-inch sticks, or if they are very small keep them whole, and cook them in no more than 2 or 3 tablespoons pure butter and an equal amount of water. Cover and cook gently; sometimes it takes no longer than 5 or 6 minutes for them to become tender. Then the cover is lifted to let the remaining water, if any, steam away. Salt, freshly ground pepper, and half a dozen or more of fresh, shredded mint leaves are added along with a few crumbs of brown sugar. Sauté a moment longer, shaking the pan. The mint flavor should be elusive, so don't add too many leaves—just enough to make guests wonder what the seasoning is.

61

## Cèpes or Mushrooms Brimond

Cook in oil at moderate heat 12 fine *cèpes* of the same size (they should be slightly hollowed out first); drain the *cèpes* and stuff with the following mixture. Chop *cèpe* stems and peelings, brown them in oil, add a finely chopped shallot, then chopped parsley and garlic, and 2 heaping tablespoons bread crumbs. Season with salt, pepper, and a little curry powder. Place the *cèpes* in a baking dish on a bed of peeled, seeded, and chopped tomatoes browned in butter. Sprinkle with bread crumbs, baste with oil, and brown in the oven at low heat.

## Green Beans Parisienne

[SERVES 4]

1 pound young green beans
3 ounces butter
4 tablespoons water
1 teaspoon lemon juice
1 teaspoon salt
½ teaspoon cayenne pepper
1 cup blanched shredded almonds
1 teaspoon chopped fresh garlic

Top and tail the beans. Cut in very thin slices diagonally. Put in cold water and bring slowly to a boil. Drain. Melt half the butter in a very heavy pan. Add the water, lemon juice, salt and pepper. Add the beans, cover and cook gently, stirring occasionally, until just soft (approximately 20 minutes). In another pan melt the rest of the butter, add the blanched shredded almonds and brown slowly. Add the chopped garlic. Put the beans in a serving dish and pour over the almonds, garlic and butter.

# Eggplants
## Provençale

Peel the eggplants and cut them in slices about ¼ inch thick; salt them and let stand 15 or 20 minutes to drain. Wipe them off, dip in flour, and sauté in a pan of oil. In another pan, sauté a few tomatoes drained and cut into pieces, add salt, pepper, and 1 or 2 chopped cloves of garlic. When the vegetables are cooked, mix them together, add some chopped parsley, and cook for a moment so that these two products of Provence blend. Serve very hot.

# Stuffed Tomatoes
## Provençale

Halve the tomatoes, remove the seeds, season, and place, open side down, in a pan containing smoking hot oil. Turn them when half cooked; let cook another moment. Lay them side by side in a baking dish and stuff with the following mixture: To stuff 6 tomatoes, brown 2 tablespoons chopped onion in oil; add 4 peeled, pressed, and crushed tomatoes, a pinch of chopped parsley, and a bit of crushed garlic; cook, covered, 12 minutes. Finish with 4 tablespoons white bread soaked in consommé and pressed through a sieve and 2 anchovies also pressed through a sieve; top off with some rather fat beef gravy. When the tomatoes are stuffed, sprinkle with bread crumbs mixed with grated cheese, baste with oil, and brown in the oven. These tomatoes may be served hot or cold.

## Tomato and Spinach Casserole

Prepare fresh or frozen spinach, chop it coarsely, sprinkle with lemon juice and 2 tablespoons sour cream, mix with it a can of button mushrooms browned in butter, and place in a casserole. On this, place several layers of sliced ripe tomatoes, each dusted with salt, pepper, and Parmesan cheese. Put a heavy layer of cheese on top, dot well with butter, and bake in a hot oven until browned. This is also fine with steak.

## Tomato- Eggplant Surprise

[SERVES 4–6]

1 small eggplant
2 or 3 medium-sized tomatoes, peeled
1 medium-sized onion, chopped
1 cup bread crumbs, sautéed in butter
¼ cup grated cheese

**BATTER**

1 egg, beaten
¼ cup milk
½ teaspoon salt
½ cup sifted flour
½ teaspoon baking powder

Slice peeled eggplant into ½-inch slices and soak 15 minutes in cold salted water. Meanwhile, prepare batter by mixing batter ingredients above. Drain eggplant thoroughly. Heat small amount of fat in skillet. Dip eggplant slices in batter, drain and fry about 3 minutes on each side. Remove from skillet and drain on paper toweling. When all slices have been fried, place half of them in a 9-inch pie plate and cover with tomato slices and chopped onion. Cover with remaining eggplant. Sprinkle with buttered bread crumbs, cheese and paprika. Bake at 350° for about 20 minutes. (May be served as a main luncheon dish or as a side dish with the meat course.)

## Zucchini Parmesan
[SERVES 6–8]

8 small zucchini
2 tablespoons olive oil
4 tablespoons butter
¼ pound Parmesan cheese, grated

Wash zucchini, cut off stem ends. Put a pot of water on to boil and add 2 tablespoons olive oil. Parboil zucchini for 10 minutes. Remove and drain. Cut zucchini in half lengthwise, place, cut side up, in buttered baking dish, sprinkle with salt and pepper and dot liberally with butter. Cover each with freshly grated Parmesan and bake in 350° oven for 15 minutes, until cheese is delicately browned.

# Potatoes, Rice and Spaghetti

## Chef's Potato Cakes

[SERVES 4]

Grate 2 cups of raw potatoes, add 2 tablespoons of onion chopped fine, a dash each of salt, pepper, thyme, and one well beaten egg. Shape into cakes and either bake on a well greased griddle or fry in deep fat.

| *Sweet Potato Soufflé* | 2 cups of mashed, cooked sweet potatoes |
| | 1 cup sour cream |
| | ¼ cup cognac |
| [SERVES 4] | 4 tablespoons melted butter |
| | ¼ teaspoon cayenne pepper |
| | ¼ teaspoon grated nutmeg |
| | ½ teaspoon salt |
| | Grated rind of half a lemon |
| | 4 egg yolks, well beaten |
| | 5 egg whites |

Put the potatoes in a bowl and gradually mix in the sour cream and cognac. Add the butter and beat the mixture until quite smooth. Beat in the cayenne pepper, nutmeg, salt and lemon rind. Then mix in the egg yolks. Beat the egg whites until very stiff and carefully fold into the mixture. Pour into a buttered soufflé dish and bake in a 400° oven for 25-30 minutes, or until lightly browned. Serve at once.

## *Boiled Potatoes in Sour Cream*

Pare 4 medium potatoes, cut into quarters, and place in a saucepan along with 1 small minced onion, salt and pepper, and water to cover. Simmer only until tender. Drain well, add 2 tablespoons butter and 4 tablespoons sour cream, cover the pan and shake gently.

## *Stuffed Baked Potatoes*

Butter
Cream
Salt and pepper
Chopped parsley
Chopped chives
Grated Parmesan cheese

Bake potatoes until just soft. With a small, sharp knife cut a slice off 1 side of each potato to make long, boat-shaped shells or barquettes. Remove insides of potatoes and put through a ricer or food mill. Combine with 1 tablespoon butter and 1 tablespoon cream for each potato, and salt and pepper to taste. Beat well. Add 1 tablespoon parsley and 1 tablespoon chives. Beat again. Refill potato shells, sprinkle with grated Parmesan cheese, and dot with butter. Return to oven just long enough for potatoes to heat through and cheese to brown lightly.

## *Wild Rice Casserole*

Boil as much wild rice as is wanted until done. Fry 4 or 5 strips of bacon until crisp, drain and crumble. In a good bit of butter, cook several chopped onions and some diced celery and parsley until transparent, but do not let it brown. Mix all together, including the butter from the pan, and add a good supply of sliced stuffed olives and some pieces of black olives. If the mixture is not moist enough, add a little broth or more melted butter. Top with browned buttered bread crumbs and heat through in a hot oven.

## *Rice and Mushroom Casserole*

3 onions, sliced
¼ pound butter
2 cups mushrooms, fresh or canned
1 cup rice
1 can consommé
1 cup water
Salt and pepper

Sauté onions and sliced mushrooms in butter. Add consommé and water. Mix well with thoroughly washed, uncooked rice. Season. Bake in greased casserole in moderate oven, 350°, 45 minutes to 1 hour.

## Gnocchi Romaine

Bring to a boil 1 quart milk with 3½ ounces butter, salt, and nutmeg. When boiling, drop in gradually 8 ounces medium semolina and stir vigorously. When the semolina is cooked and firm, mix in 1 beaten egg and grated Parmesan cheese. Mix briskly and spread on a buttered tray until ¾ inch thick. Let cool and cut into circles with a plain, round cutter. Roll them in grated Parmesan cheese, arrange in an ovenware dish, butter, and gratinate in the oven.

## Spaghetti Alfredo

[SERVES 8 AS SIDE DISH]

1 pound spaghettini (thin spaghetti)
1 stick butter
1 cup freshly grated Romano cheese

Cook spaghettini according to package directions. While it cooks, melt 1 stick (¼ pound) butter in flat dish in the oven. Pour hot, drained spaghettini into butter and toss with two forks until each strand is coated. Then add freshly grated cheese and toss again. Serve at once.

71

## Roman Spaghetti

[SERVES 6]

1½ pounds spaghetti
8 egg yolks
1 pound bacon (thick slices)
½ cup Parmesan cheese
2 tablespoons olive oil
Black pepper (coarse) to taste

Feast like a Roman emperor on this unusual spaghetti combining bacon, egg, cheese and black pepper. Be certain, however, to have all ingredients ready close at hand to combine instantly when necessary.

Boil the spaghetti for 10 or 12 minutes in 6 quarts of briskly boiling water to which a tablespoon of salt has been added. Cook until the spaghetti is slightly firm, not mushy, then drain quickly and transfer immediately to a bowl.

Meanwhile, have the slightly beaten yolks of 8 eggs ready to pour over the steaming hot spaghetti. It's very important that the spaghetti be as hot as possible at this point in order to cook the egg that coats it as it's stirred and tossed.

As soon as possible, quickly add the pound of cooked bacon (cut into ½-inch chunks) from which all the fat—except about a tablespoon—has been drained. Also add the ½ cup of Parmesan cheese and 2 tablespoons of olive oil. A dash of coarse black pepper from a pepper mill is the final touch of artistry to this masterpiece.

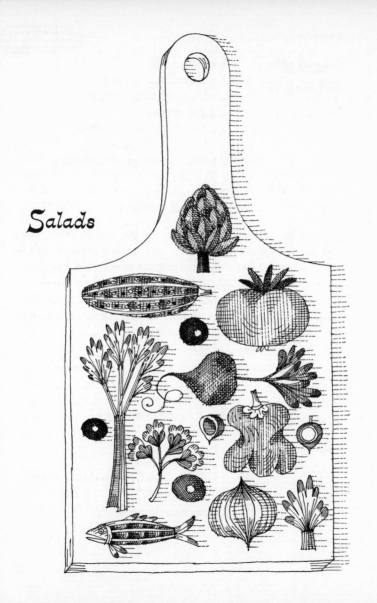

Salads

### Sour-Cream Cucumbers

[SERVES 4–6]

½ teaspoon salt
1 scant tablespoon sugar
2 tablespoons cider vinegar
1 cup sour cream
2 tablespoons chopped chives
     or a grating of onion
2 tablespoons chopped fresh dill,
     head and fronds
1 teaspoon celery seed
2 firm fresh cucumbers

Dissolve the salt and sugar in the vinegar, add the sour cream and stir smooth. You may like more or less vinegar, salt or sugar, but don't make the dressing too sweet. Add the chives, dill and celery seed. Slice the unpared cucumbers paper thin and combine with the dressing. Chill for 1 hour or more. Sour-cream cucumbers improve in taste as they stand. The flavor of the cucumbers seeps into the dressing.

### Belgian Tomatoes

[SERVES 4]

1 Spanish onion
4 well ripened tomatoes
½ teaspoon salt
¼ teaspoon sugar
Fresh ground pepper
1 tablespoon each chopped fresh chives,
     basil, dill
1 teaspoon celery seed
¼ cup French dressing

Prepare this salad on a large flat platter from which it can be served. First slice the onion and separate it into rings. Spread these on the platter. Slice the tomatoes almost ½ inch thick onto the onion rings and dust them with the salt and sugar. Sprinkle each slice with a grind of fresh pepper and chopped herbs. Sprinkle all with celery seed and French dressing. Cover the platter with aluminum foil and set it in the refrigerator to gain flavor until supper time. Serve Belgian Tomatoes with cold cuts, cheese and crusty garlic bread for a snack supper.

*Green Salad with Artichoke Hearts*

[SERVES 6]

1 lettuce
1 romaine
2-3 scallions
Small can artichoke hearts
Garlic
6 tablespoons olive oil
2 tablespoons red wine vinegar
Salt, pepper
Dry mustard
½ green pepper

Wash and dry salad greens. Mince scallions and green pepper and add. Open and drain small can artichoke hearts. Prepare dressing by crushing garlic with salt, adding olive oil, red wine vinegar, pepper, and pinch of mustard if wanted. Stir well, pour over salad, and toss.

75

### Romaine Caesar Salad

[SERVES 4–6]

1 clove garlic
6 anchovy fillets
3 tablespoons Parmesan cheese
1 egg
3 tablespoons olive oil
1 tablespoon wine vinegar
4 slices bread, cut thin
2 tablespoons butter
2 heads of romaine

Mash the garlic in a large wooden salad bowl, rubbing it well around the sides. Let it stand thus for a few minutes, then scrape out and discard the garlic pulp. Put the anchovy fillets and cheese into the bowl and mash them to a smooth paste. Coddle the egg by cooking it in fast-boiling water for one minute, just enough to cut the edge of rawness. Add this to the anchovy-cheese mixture and work smooth. Blend in the oil and vinegar. Neither salt nor pepper is needed.

Make croutons by buttering the bread on both sides, cubing it small, and browning the croutons in the oven until crisp.

Wash the romaine well, dry and crisp it. Break it into the bowl, sprinkle on the croutons and toss lightly in the dressing until every leaf is coated and the dressing absorbed by the croutons.

For a memorable outdoor meal on a warm summer evening, serve an outsize bowl of Caesar Salad with grilled steak sandwiches followed by peach shortcake.

In doubling or tripling this recipe, you can put all the ingredients for the dressing into a blender (cutting the amount of garlic in half) for a quick whirl. Store the dressing in a screw-cap jar until the salad is ready to be tossed. The flavor is the same, but the texture of the dressing is creamy and looks less attractive on the romaine.

## Celery-Root Salad

Cut the celery root in thin julienne strips and season with thin mayonnaise strongly flavored with mustard.

## Salad with Anchovy

1 lettuce
1 romaine
Watercress
Small can anchovy fillets
4 tablespoons olive oil
1 tablespoon lemon juice
Salt, pepper
1 clove garlic, crushed

Wash and dry lettuce and romaine and break into serving pieces into salad bowl. Keep watercress on ice until just before serving, then wash and strip leaves from stems. Add leaves to salad greens. Drain can of anchovy fillets, wash under warm running water, snip into bits. Prepare salad dressing from other ingredients, add anchovy bits, stir well, and pour over salad greens. Toss and serve.

## Red-Cabbage
## Salad

Take very tender red cabbage; separate the leaves and cut in thin julienne strips. Season with oil and vinegar at least 6 hours before serving.

| *Beet Velvet*<br>*Mold* | 1 package lemon gelatin |
|---|---|

*Beet Velvet*
*Mold*

1 package lemon gelatin
1 cup hot water
2 4½-ounce cans strained baby-food beets
½ pint sour cream
1 tablespoon lemon juice
1 teaspoon grated onion
⅛ teaspoon MSG (monosodium
glutamate)
Salt and pepper

Dissolve gelatin in hot water and allow to cool. Add all ingredients, mix, and pour into oiled mold. Chill. Serve with sour-cream dressing.

78

# Desserts and Dessert Beverages

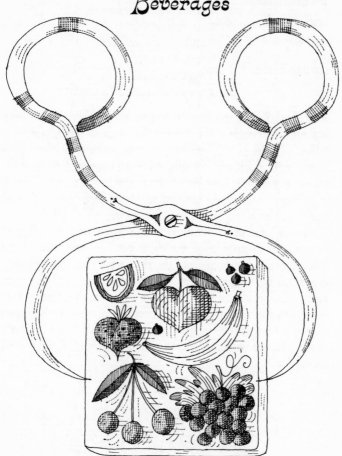

## Mocha Icebox Cake and Mocha Filling

[SERVES 8–10]

2½ dozen lady fingers
1 cup hot milk
3 tablespoons instant coffee
½ cup sugar
2 tablespoons cornstarch
⅛ teaspoon salt
3 eggs, separated
1 teaspoon vanilla

Pour the hot milk over coffee and let stand where it will keep hot for 10 minutes. Mix cornstarch, salt and sugar in double boiler, add the yolks, well beaten, and stir in the coffee. Cook slowly until thick and smooth; while still warm, fold in stiffly beaten egg whites. Line bottom and sides of a spring form with lady fingers, separated, rounded side toward the pan and close together. Cut off end for ease in setting up.

Place a layer of the filling in form on lady fingers, on top of this arrange another layer of lady fingers, another layer of the filling and so on, according to the size of the form, placing lady fingers on top like spokes of a wheel. Chill overnight or until firm. When ready to serve, remove rim of spring form, place cake with tin bottom on platter, cover top with the whipped cream, adding while whipping, confectioners' sugar to taste and ½ teaspoon vanilla. Decorate with pistachio nuts, or candied cherries, cut.

*Devil's Food Cake*

¼ cup butter
1 cup sugar
2 eggs, well beaten
1½ cups flour
1½ teaspoons baking powder
½ teaspoon salt
½ cup thick, sour milk
2 ounces chocolate, melted, or 2
        tablespoons cocoa
½ cup boiling coffee
1 teaspoon soda
1 teaspoon vanilla

Preheat oven to 350°, a moderate oven. Cream butter, add sugar gradually, beat until very light. Add eggs. Beat thoroughly. Add flour mixed with baking powder alternately with the sour milk, a small amount at a time. Pour boiling coffee over melted chocolate and mix quickly. To this add the soda and stir until cool. Cool slightly, then add to cake batter. Add vanilla and mix thoroughly. Bake in two well greased 9-inch layer-cake pans for about 25 minutes, or in 8-inch square loaf pan. Fill and frost with chocolate or marshmallow frosting.

81

### Linzer Torte

1 cup butter
2 cups sifted flour
¼ teaspoon salt
1 generous cup powdered sugar
1 cup ground almonds
½ teaspoon cinnamon
¼ teaspoon allspice
1 teaspoon cocoa
½ lemon
3 egg yolks

Knead together butter, flour, salt, powdered sugar, almonds, cinnamon, allspice, cocoa, the juice and grated rind of ½ lemon, and egg yolks. When thoroughly blended, chill. Then roll ⅔ of the dough ¼ inch thick and line a spring form, giving it a good edge. Spread the dough generously with raspberry jam. Roll remaining dough into strips ¼ inch wide and place criss-cross over jam. Then place one wide strip around cake edge. Paint dough with egg white, slightly beaten. Bake in a moderate oven (350°) 45 to 55 minutes. When cool, fill squares formed by the lattice with more jam and sprinkle with powdered sugar.

### Cream Puffs

[MAKES 12 LARGE PUFFS]

½ cup butter
1 cup water
1 cup flour
4 eggs, unbeaten

Heat butter and water. When butter is melted, add flour all at once and stir vigorously until mixture no longer sticks to sides of pan. Remove from stove; cool slightly; add eggs one at a time, beating after each egg is added. Drop by heaping tablespoons onto a well greased baking sheet. Place 2 inches apart and bake in hot oven, 450°, 20 minutes. Reduce heat to 325°, and bake about 20 minutes longer. Remove from baking sheet and cool. When ready to serve, cut open on one side, and fill with whipped cream.

These are always a good standby, simple to make, and delicious, too, filled with vanilla custard, or filled with ice cream and topped with chocolate sauce.

## Chocolate Angel Pie

[SERVES 6–8]

3 egg whites
Dash of salt
⅛ teaspoon cream of tartar
¾ cup sifted sugar
¾ cup ground blanched almonds
1 teaspoon almond extract
¼ pound sweet chocolate
3 tablespoons brewed coffee
1 tablespoon cognac
1 cup heavy cream

Beat the egg whites until foamy. Add the salt and cream of tartar. Beat until peaks form. Beat in the sugar, a spoonful at a time, beating until stiff. Fold in the almonds and extract. Pile on the bottom and sides of a 9-inch buttered pie plate. Bake in a 275° oven for 45 minutes or until firm and lightly browned. Cool. Melt the chocolate in the coffee. Add the cognac, stirring until smooth. Whip the cream and fold in the chocolate mixture thoroughly. Pour into the prepared pie plate. Chill at least 3 hours before serving.

*Chocolate*
*Torte*

¼ pound sweet chocolate
2 tablespoons water
¼ pound butter
⅔ cup sugar
3 egg yolks
⅔ cup ground almonds
⅔ cup sifted cake flour
3 egg whites, stiffly beaten
1 cup heavy cream, whipped

Melt the chocolate in the water. Preheat the oven to 325°. Butter an 8-inch square pan and dust it lightly with flour.

Cream the butter, gradually adding the sugar, egg yolks and chocolate. Mix very well. Add almonds and beat well again. Add the flour, mixing lightly. Fold in the egg whites thoroughly.

Bake 35 minutes, or until a cake tester comes out clean. Cool.

Serve with the whipped cream, flavored with 2 tablespoons cocoa and 2 tablespoons sugar, if desired.

*Apricot*
*Soufflé*

[SERVES 6]

2 tablespoons butter
3 level tablespoons flour
¾ cup milk
2 teaspoons lemon juice
½ cup apricot jam or 1 cup cooked
apricot pulp
4 egg yolks
4 tablespoons sugar
5 egg whites, beaten stiff
Confectioners' sugar

Melt butter and stir in flour off fire. When blended, pour on milk. Stir over fire until thick; it must not boil. Then add lemon juice and apricot jam or cooked apricot pulp. Mix in egg yolks and sugar, and lastly fold in beaten egg whites.

Grease an 8-inch soufflé dish. Dust with sugar and tie wax paper outside to form a cuff. Fill with mixture and bake for ½ hour in a 350° oven. Remove paper, dust with confectioners' sugar and serve immediately.

## Peach Torte

[SERVES 6–8]

Whoever bears this festive torte away from our village bake sale is considered by all the winner. Mix together with the hands ½ pound butter, 2 tablespoons sugar, a pinch of salt and 2½ cups flour. Press this rich dough into the bottom and sides of a spring form and bake about ¾ hour in a 350° oven, watching that it does not burn. This shell should be baked the day before it is wanted. On the following day, drain 1 quart canned peaches well, and place the fruit in the shell. Pour over them a custard made of 3 egg yolks and 1 cup milk in which 1 tablespoon cornstarch has been dissolved, boiled together until thick. Beat the egg whites stiff, add 4 tablespoons sugar and dot the top of the torte with this generously. Bake in a slow oven until light brown.

*Filbert Torte*

[SERVES 8]

8 egg yolks
1½ cups confectioners' sugar
½ cup bread crumbs
1 lemon, grated rind
Juice of ½ lemon
½ pound grated filberts or hazelnuts
8 egg whites, beaten stiff

Preheat oven to 325°, a moderate oven. Beat yolks and sugar until very light, add bread crumbs and the rest of the ingredients in order, the beaten whites last. Bake in a greased and floured 9-inch spring form for 40 to 45 minutes. Decorate with a frosting and nuts.

Or, bake in two layers, with fresh strawberries, or sweetened whipped cream, between and on top of cake.

*Frozen Chocolate Pudding*

[SERVES 6]

1 cup sugar
4 tablespoons cornstarch
2 cups scalded milk
⅛ teaspoon salt
2 teaspoons vanilla
1 cup heavy cream
2 squares bitter chocolate or ¼ cup cocoa

Mix sugar and cornstarch, add the scalded milk gradually, and cook over hot water for 10 minutes, stirring constantly. Add the chocolate, melted or grated. Cool, add the vanilla, and fold in the cream, whipped stiff. Pour into a mold, or in trays of mechanical refrigerator. Freeze.

## Lemon Pie

2 cups plus 2 teaspoons flour
½ cup oil
¼ cup cold milk
½ teaspoon salt
3 eggs
¼ teaspoon cream of tartar
1 package lemon pie mix
⅔ cup sugar, *also* 6 tablespoons sugar
2 tablespoons butter
2 tablespoons lemon juice
1¾ cups water
Grated rind of 1 lemon

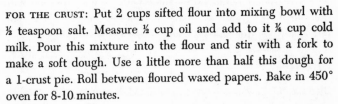

FOR THE CRUST: Put 2 cups sifted flour into mixing bowl with ½ teaspoon salt. Measure ½ cup oil and add to it ¼ cup cold milk. Pour this mixture into the flour and stir with a fork to make a soft dough. Use a little more than half this dough for a 1-crust pie. Roll between floured waxed papers. Bake in 450° oven for 8-10 minutes.

FOR THE FILLING: Separate 3 eggs. Add yolks to 1 package lemon pie mix along with ⅔ cup sugar and 1¾ cups water. Cook this mixture over medium flame until it boils and thickens, about 5 minutes. Let cool slightly, then add 2 tablespoons butter, 2 tablespoons lemon juice, and the grated rind. Stir well, pour into baked pie shell.

FOR THE MERINGUE: Beat 3 egg whites until stiff with ¼ teaspoon cream of tartar, adding 6 tablespoons sugar, 1 tablespoon at a time. Beat until meringue forms peaks when beater is lifted out. Spoon carefully over filling and swirl. Bake at 425° until swirls are golden.

*Cream Cheese*
*Torte*

[SERVES 8–10]

4 eggs
1 cup sugar
1 tablespoon lemon juice
4 8-ounce packages cream cheese
Zwieback or graham cracker crust

Line a spring form with the crust reserving ¼ cup of crumbs. Preheat oven to 375°, a moderate oven. Beat eggs, sugar, and lemon juice until light. Add the cheese to the mixture and beat thoroughly. Pour filling into crust and bake for 30 minutes. Remove torte from oven; increase oven heat to 475°, a hot oven. While torte is hot, top with 2 cups sour cream mixed with 1 teaspoon vanilla and 4 tablespoons sugar. Sprinkle with the remaining crumbs and bake 10 minutes longer. When cool, put in refrigerator and let stand a day before serving.

## CRUST

Blend 2 cups zwieback or graham cracker crumbs with 4 tablespoons confectioners' sugar and ½ cup melted butter. Spread and press mixture on buttered sides and bottom of spring form. Chill for several hours.

## Strawberries Supreme

Wash, hull, and slice 1 quart ripe strawberries. Add 2 cups sugar and allow berries to stand an hour. Heat gently over low heat and allow berries to come to the boil and boil 1 minute. Remove from fire and allow to cool thoroughly. Serve with vanilla ice cream, and add whipped cream which has been flavored with orange curaçao.

## Orangeade Cake

¾ cup butter
1 cup sugar
2 eggs
2¼ cups flour
1 teaspoon baking powder
1 teaspoon soda
½ cup seedless raisins (optional)
2 oranges, grated rind
1 cup pecans, chopped
1 cup sour milk or cream

Preheat oven to 350°, a moderate oven. Cream butter well, add sugar gradually. Beat until light and fluffy. Add eggs 1 at a time, beating well. Sift 2 cups flour, baking powder and soda. Add alternately with milk to the butter mixture. Mix rest of flour with raisins, nuts, and grated rind, add to dough and stir until smooth. Bake 1 hour in a 9-inch greased tube pan. When done, immediately pour 1 cup of orange juice with ½ cup sugar over cake. Let stand in pan until cool.

### Café Serendip

[SERVES 1]

½ cup espresso coffee
½ cup hot milk
Bit of grated orange peel
Nutmeg

Put coffee and milk in tall cup or mug. It would be wise to pre-heat the receptacle. Top with the grated orange peel and dash of nutmeg. Also, if you desire, with a blob of whipped cream.

### Russian Chocolate

[SERVES 4]

1 ounce cooking chocolate
¼ cup sugar
⅛ teaspoon salt
1¾ cups boiling water
½ cup milk
½ cup heavy cream
1 teaspoon vanilla
2 cups hot, freshly made coffee

Melt chocolate in top of double boiler and add sugar, salt, and boiling water. Stir and cook 5 minutes. Add milk and cream, reheat, but do not allow to come to a boil. Add vanilla and coffee. Beat mixture well with an egg beater until frothy, and serve at once.

*Irish Coffee*

[SERVES 1]

½ teaspoon sugar
1 jigger Irish whisky
Hot coffee
1 tablespoon sweetened whipped cream

Put sugar and whisky in bottom of short-stemmed glass. Pour coffee until glass is ⅔ full. Add whipped cream and, if you like, dust lightly with nutmeg, and serve.

# Index